IT MADE
SENSE

IT MADE
A DIFFERENCE

CHRISTIAN FOCUS

It Made

SENSE

for some - it made sense!
for some - it made a difference!
for many others - it did both!

It Made

A DIFFERENCE

some stories of lives that have been
changed as a result of the Evangelism
Explosion training programme

© Evangelism Explosion
ISBN 1 85792 5998

Published in 2000
by
Christian Focus Publications, Geanies House,
Fearn, Ross-shire, IV20 1TW, Great Britain

www.christianfocus.com

Cover design by Alister MacInnes

Printed by Cox & Wyman Ltd,
Reading, Berkshire

Contents

Contents

INTRODUCTION

*'by setting forth the truth plainly
we commend ourselves to every
man's conscience'* (2 Cor. 4:2b)

It is a Christians' **birthright** to win souls for Christ, but less than 5% of the members of most churches have ever had that privilege. That does not reflect a lack of zeal on the part of those 95%, but rather a lack of training. No one has ever shown them how they can share their faith with others so that it makes sense, or how to proceed if it does!

In spite of what we may feel **should** be the case, the task of making disciples is a skill for which most of us need training. Jesus was the best Bible teacher the world will ever see, but He did not rely on his teaching and preaching. He gave his men practical on-the-job training. Then, once they had been empowered by the Holy Spirit, they not only had the zeal to tell the good news but also the practical training for its application. That formula still holds good today.

Since the early 1960s Evangelism Explosion has demonstrated that when Christians are shown how to witness, **they do!** As presenters of the gospel message that *practical training* 'makes a difference' and for the person on the receiving end, the message 'makes sense'. Of course not all who hear, receive – that is the work of the Holy Spirit – but those witnesses can rest in the knowledge that they have set forth the truth plainly.

The stories contained in this booklet bear witness to these and other aspects of this most effective training ministry.

If you haven't used EE I would urge you to try it for yourself. It does make sense and whatever your theological training it will make a difference.

Peter Crook, National Director EE(GB)

1

Preaching with a difference

One-on-one evangelism is not everyone's cup of tea. Some of us find it difficult to converse with people we've never met let alone tell them about Jesus. Yes, as Christians we know that we are supposed to evangelise and therefore we try occasionally, but in the main we let the evangelists do the work. Surely God calls particular people to be evangelists doesn't he?

This was my rationale for the first twenty years of ministry. After all, I reasoned, God called me to be a Bible teacher not an evangelist; and though I never mentioned it, I felt decidedly uncomfortable *trying* to persuade strangers or even friends to accept Jesus as Lord. There was one very embarrassing afternoon in the summer of '81 after I had just received my degree in theology and was with a Youth for Christ team on the streets of Bristol. I finally worked up the boldness to speak to some people, but no one responded. It made me feel depressed, and I decided I would not do that again. If God wanted me to win people to the Lord, He would have to put them in front of me and keep them there while He inspired me to speak.

Ten years later as ministry opportunities opened up in Eastern Europe and then Asia my perception of evangelism began to change. Though I was primarily involved with Bible teaching, the opportunity would occasionally arise to make a call for repentance which I would do based on my personal testimony, and most of the unsaved would come forward. Nevertheless it was not something I particularly enjoyed because I was never sure whether people would respond or not and was always slightly surprised when they did. Probably three or four hundred souls were saved over the next few years in this manner, but I still did not consider my role as anything more than a Bible teacher.

Then in August of 1995 something rather amazing happened. I had been asked to develop a syllabus for a missionary training school in Siberia and had completed all the teaching outlines except the part on evangelism. As I walked in the fields behind my home early one morning, I asked God what I should do about this segment of the syllabus. I told Him I would make my own outline or use any other one He might recommend. He did not answer in words, rather He showed me why He loved Jim Kennedy.

I had known Dr. D. James Kennedy and Evangelism Explosion since becoming a

Christian almost twenty years earlier because Jim is my brother's pastor (back in Florida). But I had never been interested in the EE concept and had therefore not considered it for the mission school syllabus. So this rather amazing revelation of God's love for Jim Kennedy was completely unexpected. Nevertheless, as I meditated on God's response I knew EE was the course He wanted me to use, so I signed up for the next available 6-day Leader's Training Course. On completion of that course the emphasis in my ministry began to change as God's hand gently led me in a new and very rewarding direction.

My next trip abroad was early in the following year to the Philippines where I had been invited to teach at a Pastor's Training School in Manila. The morning after we arrived I was asked to speak in a Sunday service. There was a group of about ten young people sitting apart from the rest, and for some reason I felt inspired to make a call for repentance. The entire group came forward. The pastor said they had never been in the church before. After the service he asked if I would go into a squatters village and tell people about Jesus. I did not want to do that, but he was my host so I said, yes. We went later that week and I spoke about the Lord to those who cared to listen. Twenty-five people came forward for salvation. The following week I spoke in that village again and another forty-five received Jesus including an entire drug gang. It was an exhilarating experience!

Shortly thereafter I went back to Siberia to do some teaching. While there I was asked to speak in the community hall of a village where my host had been struggling to start a church. I gave a short message, made a call for repentance and everybody came forward. It surprised and really encouraged me.

The following Autumn we returned to Siberia and conducted the missionary training programme which I had been preparing when God revealed to me His love for Jim Kennedy. Because of the complexity of the language I decided to bring in an EE trainer from Uzbekistan. It was a great success and we saw a number of souls saved and two new churches planted. Evangelism was beginning to excite me, EE seemed to be effective in every situation.

It was about this time that I began to hear God *urging* me to preach the gospel to the poor. I had always wanted to preach the gospel to the rich, so this is not what I was eager to hear. Nevertheless as I looked back over the past twenty years I realised that preaching the gospel to the poor had been God's direction for my ministry from the very beginning, but now I was experiencing something new. A compassion I had never felt was being birthed deep in my heart for this forgotten majority which comprises about 60% of the world's population.

Nevertheless I felt it necessary to test the vision, so I put together some teaching notes and organised a couple of three-day Pastors' seminars early the next year entitled 'Ministry To The Poor'. The first of these was held in Manila with thirty pastors in attendance. We only had time for a single crusade after the seminar, so we decided on one of one of the worst and most dangerous of the squatters' villages and held an impromptu meeting right in the very heart of it. One hundred-forty people including forty children came to the Lord! My host said later, *'You are more than a teacher, you are an evangelist and should be holding big crusades. The message you gave tonight contained everything necessary for people to understand their need for Jesus.'* When I told him that I had simply used the EE method he and many of the other pastors wanted to attend a Leaders' Training Course, but unfortunately they could not afford the cost. A week later I held the second seminar in another area followed by crusades and two hundred more souls were saved. Again the pastors were very impressed by the EE method but could not afford the cost of the course. Now, with Dr Kennedy's permission, the EE presentation is incorporated in the Pastor's Manual, which we distribute without charge to those who attend.

I returned to the Philippines early the following year (1998) and spent several months conducting 3-day Pastor's Seminars which were attended by over 200 pastors. We held twenty-three crusades and 2,500 people received Jesus. Two of these crusades were held in the squatters villages which we had previously visited. In the first village there are now over 300 Christians and the second has more than 500! About half of these are children.

I came back to England after three months, but the Filipino pastors that we trained began to hold their own seminars using our Pastor's Manual which they photocopy and give away. At the time of writing this another 500 persons (not including children) have come to the Lord in a dozen crusades; and more seminars and crusades are planned for early 1999.

Did the EE course which I attended in 1995 have an appreciable effect on my ministry...and on my life? The simple answer is, yes, most assuredly! In fact whenever I am invited to speak at non-Christian and even Christian functions I generally conclude with the EE presentation and the unsaved come forward. Since attending that course, almost 4,000 people have come to the

Lord through this ministry, which is an average of one thousand souls a year (almost three a day); and the figures are rising. Because many of the pastors we initially trained are continuing to bring people to the Lord, revival is beginning to break out in some of the areas we pioneered! Now I am praying for more doors to open in other nations of the world.

I'm still just a Bible teacher, but I've got an anointed tool that really gets the attention of the lost. It's called EE and it really makes a difference.

Alex Forbes (BD)
Alex lives with his wife in Henfield, Sussex from where he heads up the Embassy Christian Outreach Fund, an evangelistic Bible teaching and training ministry.

2

Mountain top experiences from a church in the valley

Abertridwr is a small village just outside of Caerphilly in South Wales. It is predominantly a working-class community and has a population of around three and a half thousand people.

Our Community Church has been using the EE training programme since March 1983 and as a direct result many, many lives in our community have been touched and changed. There have been disappointments of course, which are to expected in evangelism, but there have also been many successes. We get so excited by the blessing of people coming to the Lord. Here are just a few of the countless stories that could be told.

The first person who came to the Lord through EE in 1983 was Cheryl. She was married with two children and typical of so many people today. Her marriage had run into difficulty, and she felt that there was something missing in her life, but didn't know what it was. Then, one Wednesday afternoon in May an EE team visited her. When the gospel was presented, it made so much sense that she asked the Lord into her life. From that day to this, she has never looked back. She has gone through the programme herself, and has had the joy of leading others to Christ. Cheryl is currently one of our prayer co-ordinators in the church.

One evening a team visited the home of a young couple, Ken and Ann. Ken wasn't at home, but after making friends with Ann, the team presented the gospel to her. The Lord opened her heart in the same way that Lydia's heart was opened in the Bible. When asked, 'Are you willing to put your trust in Jesus Christ, repent of sin, and receive God's gift of eternal life?' she enthusiastically said, yes. Then, just as she was about to pray a prayer of response, the door opened and in walked Ken. *'What's going on here?'* asked Ken. The leader of the team explained to him that the gospel had been shared with his wife, and that she was about to pray. Ken remarked, *'Well, before she prays you had better tell me what you've told her'.* The gospel was then presented a second time, and the team had the joy of leading both husband and wife to the Lord. Today Ken is a leader of one of our house groups, and they are both going on with the Lord.

Then there is Brian. Brian was a spiritualist medium who was in constant demand throughout

South Wales and the West country. He was always fully booked to go somewhere at least six months in advance. He had practised as a medium for a number of years, then one day he decided to stop. He says: *'At that time I didn't know why, but now I know that the Lord was in it, he was preparing me for what was going to be a life-changing experience.'* Subsequently, Brian married Margaret – a member of our church. She trained in EE and many times Margaret persuaded Brian to receive a visit from a team so that they could practice what they were learning. He soon came to know the most of the presentation and would correct a trainee if he or she made a mistake. He called himself a 'professional' listener. But God says 'His word shall not return to him void' and without knowing it Brian was being brought under conviction. He now admits that many times after a team left he would feel quite uncomfortable, but didn't know why.

Although Brian had stopped being a medium it was still in his mind and spirit, and he couldn't shake it off. His marriage eventually got into difficulty and began to go down hill until they were legally separated. Just a week before filing for divorce an EE team visited them. Again the gospel was presented to him but on this occasion it made sense! In his despair, Brian reached out and took the gift of eternal life. He renounced spiritualism and all that he had practised, and asked the Lord into his life. The Holy Spirit worked in Brian that day, and he just wept and wept as wave after wave of God's love broke upon him. In fact he wept for many days as the love of God touched his life. Today, Brian has a great compassion for people who are hurting, and has a deep desire to help and care for such people.

One humorous and unique story involved a visit to the home of a middle-aged couple. They were very friendly and gave the team a warm welcome. The evening visit was going well, when suddenly the door burst open and in came their son. He was very distraught because his wife-to-be had run away. There was such a commotion. It resulted in the mother, father and son rushing out of the house. The mother turned as she went, and said to the team, close the door behind you when you leave. They just looked at each other in amazement. But again this humorous story has a happy ending. The wife-to-be returned home, and the couple got married. But most importantly, the couple visited, namely Don and Margaret both came to the Lord, and are still worshipping with us today.

Then there was Julie, she was a drug addict and alcoholic. Left to fend for herself from an early age, she was suspicious of everyone, she never knew the meaning of true love. If anyone tried to get close to her in her mind there was an ulterior motive behind it, and they were probably after something. Her philosophy for life was simple, do it to them before they do it to you!

She is a single parent, with three children, and one of them, a lovely little girl, is disabled. One big hang up Julie had was a hatred toward all men, this was understandable because they had so often used and abused her in the past.

Then one day she was visited by Jean, a member of our church who worked for the Social Services. She sought to help Julie in the bringing up of her children and visited her regularly for eighteen months. During the course of one visit Jean heard screaming and cursing coming from the back of the house. She rushed around horrified to find Julie about to hit her neighbour over the head with a hammer because of something she had said to her daughter. Jean stepped in and calmed the situation down. She told Julie that she attended church and invited her to come. Julie attended church the following Sunday for the first time in her life.

Eventually two teams went to visit her on a Wednesday evening. One team was allocated the task of looking after the children, the other had the responsibility of presenting the gospel to Julie. It was a bizarre evening; all sorts of people

21

kept coming and going, with Julie leaving us at regular intervals to go into the kitchen. We found out later that those 'excursions' were to smoke a 'joint'! But the incredible happened! The gospel was presented and she agreed that it made sense. She was then asked if she was prepared to repent of her sin, turn away from her destructive lifestyle and receive God's gift of eternal life. To the team's amazement she said, 'Yes'.

As you can imagine she brought much 'baggage from the past' with her into the church. She needed a great deal of help, and many hours have been spent with her as bit by bit all the rubbish of her past life is being removed. She's now showing to her friends old and new, that she is **'a new creation in Christ, and that the old had gone and the new has come'.**

Another blessing and spin-off effect of EE is that it can unearth an evangelistic gift in a person. One such person is Cynthia. She was one of the first two people trained at our church. As an active Sunday School superintendent and youth worker she was very reluctant to stop these activities in order to be trained. Eventually she was persuaded to do so. On completing the programme she had a new found passion, a desire to share her faith with others. This she has continued to do for nearly sixteen years, and has led a number of people to the Lord.

These are just a few success stories, there are many more and as a church we thank God for Evangelism Explosion. It does make a difference, and brings a great deal of excitement and freshness as a result of the 'new life' of those coming to faith.

Since we started EE in 1983 we have completed nineteen local church programmes and held ten Leaders Training Courses. During this time seventy five people from the church have been trained, and well over two hundred people have attended the Leaders' Training Courses.

Many in our church are now able to confidently share their faith with others and through EE they have been taught how to effectively disciple these new believers. Our church has grown by about six hundred percent, largely through this effective tool, and we shall continue to use it in the future.

Rev Bryan Alexander,
Bryan lives with his wife Jean and one of his daughters in Abertridwr, near Caerphilly, where he is the senior minister of the Community Church. Bryan is also a member of the Board of Directors of EE(GB).

3

A repair man with a difference!

I was trained in EE on a six-day Leaders'
Training Course in 1998. I remember quite
vividly the first day I heard the course advertised
on Premier Radio. I was very excited about it as
I discussed it with my wife because it sounded
like just the very thing I wanted to do, and we
had been praying for. I could not wait to start
the course, and was so eager that I turned up a
day early at the church – only to discover that I
was alone in the building. The course did not
start until the next day. I was so overwhelmed
by the whole thing that I did not have time to be
embarrassed.

On the first day of the course, when we got
the folder which contained the course work, I
was very shocked to see how much work we had
to cover in such a short time – all the scriptures
and the illustrations we had to remember. At that
moment I thought I would not be able to finish
the course in just six days.

But as the teaching got under way my eyes
began to open to a lot of questions that I had
been asking, which no-one had been able to give
me answers to before. For example, the

presentation of the gospel in a structured way so as to give each Christian a base from which they can work when sharing their faith. I had always struggled to find the right words whenever I witnessed. At the end of that first day I began to feel more relaxed because I realised that this course contained everything that I wanted to learn.

I went home that evening and started my homework straight away. After an hour of study I realised that if I just stuck to it, and did not give up, I would not have any problems. I did and it turned out to be one of the best courses I have even done in all my life. Evangelism Explosion has given me something that no-one can take away, but I am always ready share it or give it away!

On the last day of the course there was to be a 'banquet' in the evening to celebrate the end of the course. I went home to collect my wife for the banquet and on the way back to the church I visited one of my customers to pick up some money owed to me. As I went into the house, I saw two young ladies. I introduced myself to them and began to share with them what I had learned on the EE course. Instantly I had their attention. As they listened to me, I could see that they were really interested and especially when I moved into the gospel presentation they were very impressed. I also was so impressed by their patience that I completely forgot the money I went there to get in the first place. Before I left that house both young ladies and their mother made a commitment to our Lord Jesus. Isn't that exciting?

On a recent occasion I went to fix a washing machine for another customer. After completing the job, I left the house, forgetting a piece of board about 2 feet long. I had used the board to help knock out the washing machine bearings. This piece of board was not important to me, however, for two days, I felt the Holy Spirit telling me to go back for it. Finally, I decided to go back and as I rang the bell, a young man came to open the door. I had not seen him on my first visit. I felt the Holy Spirit encouraging me to share the gospel with him. So, having made friends with him I shared the gospel, it made sense and he gladly made a commitment to Christ – Hallelujah! Ten minutes later his father came downstairs and told me that both he and his wife were Christians and for years they had been trying to get this young man to church but he had always been rebellious. Isn't God wonderful?

During a recent Sunday morning service at our church I met a young man and asked him if he had truly made a commitment to God. He told me sincerely that he had not; so I shared the gospel with him – EE style – and he was amazed. He told me he had never heard the gospel presented so simply and so clearly. He immediately made a commitment to Christ. He was so overwhelmed he started to cry. He was so happy and began to pray and thank God for his salvation. To God be the Glory, great things He has done. I realised that I should not take it for granted that everyone who comes to church has an assurance in Christ for the salvation.

Evangelism Explosion has made such a great impact on my life. With its real Bible study, its practical evangelism and the commitment needed to make it work, my life has not been the same since I finished the course. It has made me confident, competent and bold and it has also changed my character. I am more concerned for unsaved souls and my compassion has increased for those that are lost. I am so happy to have been equipped with the right tools. No longer do I have to struggle for words when I am sharing my faith with friends at work, or with neighbours, because I have the Word of God in my heart and in my mouth. I have never used anything as effective as Evangelism Explosion.

I told my pastor about Evangelism Explosion and he saw the difference it made in my life. He now wants me to train every House Group in the church.

To-date – by the leading of the Holy Spirit –
I have led 28 people to Christ (Praise God!).
Please pray for me that I will continue to make
disciples for Christ by the power of the Holy
Spirit and the knowledge I have received from
the Evangelism Explosion training course. Please
pray also for my family that they will continue
to support me as I spend time to disciple new
converts. My wife now also uses Evangelism
Explosion at her work place to share her faith.

It is good to *know how* to be fishers of men
but it is better to *catch* them for Jesus.

Dennis Webber
Dennis lives in North London with his wife
Patsy. Dennis is a member of Emmanuel
Christian Centre, London E17, where, amongst
other things, he is responsible for teaching the
EE programme.

4

Prepared to make a difference

Going on the EE Leaders Training Course was one of the hardest things I have ever done. But I was so excited at the prospect that I might be able to lead people to Christ that by God's grace I managed to get through. I am so glad that I did, for I am equipped and ready.....

The tube doors slammed shut on the Circle Line and we were on our way, myself and the little old lady in the woollen head scarf with the perky face and the Cockney accent, heading east – at last. It was a quiet Saturday morning on the London underground and the trains seemed to have been as asleep as the people. In my anxiety to keep my appointment, I had struck up a conversation with this little person 'Were the trains actually running?' During the quarter of an hour wait our talk had drifted from the dearth of trains to global warming, and now, settled comfortably in the train, I was learning that this gentle independent soul was on her way to visit her sister. She was a widow. She had married during the Second World War and immediately her husband had gone away with his regiment.

He had one week's leave and during that week he had been run over by a car on a London street. That had been the end of her marriage. My heart went out with compassion at the irony of this story, but I saw no self pity or anger in her eyes.

Only one stop to go. I wanted to give something to this lady, to make up for all the lonely stoical years that had been her life. But what to give? My experience had been so much happier. I couldn't begin to understand her situation. I had only one gift to offer, and only four minutes within which to pass it on. Up went a silent prayer, 'Lord, speak through me, this is your work – help me share the crucial parts of the outline' Then, out loud, 'Excuse me, but may I ask you a question?' 'Oh no dearie, I won't go to heaven!'

It could only have been four minutes later that I was standing up to jump out of those doors and race up the stairs. The train was drawing to a halt. 'I won't see you again, at least not this side of heaven', I said desperately, 'but maybe we'll meet in heaven?' I questioned. 'Oh yes dear, she said emphatically, 'and I'll know you!' I felt a rush of joy for I knew that she meant it. She had taken in every word and somehow miraculously I had left no part of the gospel story out. In my rush, however, I failed to find a copy of 'Just Grace'.

I had been better organised a year earlier when heading once again for an appointment in central London. This time I had a quarter of an hour to spare. I sent up a prayer – 'Use this time for your glory, Lord' As I prayed, my heart turned to shopping and I headed toward my favourite department store! This would be fun! 'Thank you Lord'.

Big Issue – Big Issue' was the cry I heard behind me. I was already ten paces beyond and I had no intention of stopping – after all I only had a quarter of an hour. But I could not proceed. I turned round and started to retrace my steps, my eyes firmly to the ground. I didn't want to buy the Big Issue and certainly didn't want to get involved with its salesman.

'*I will buy the Big Issue after all*' I said stoically and gave him my change, all of 80p. There was something about his meek response that touched my Dives heart of stone. '*It's all right*' he said. 'What was all right?' He didn't say anything. (The Big Issue costs £1.00.) '*Its all right*' he insisted, '*it doesn't matter, please have it anyway.*' Somehow he had become the donor, and I the penitent. '*I'm so sorry, I'm so sorry*' I said. I felt such a hypocrite. Here was this boy making a gift of 20p to me so I could have a magazine that I did not want. What could I give him of any value in return?

I usually find that I am neck deep in these improbable situations before I recognise God's hand of appointment. Yes, I could give two things, my time and the greatest gift ever given.

The young man, Stephen, listened in awe as we went through the gospel. He had not heard it before and at the end he gratefully prayed to receive the gift of eternal life. His nights were spent in a hostel and his days on this street. How would he get into a church that would suit him? I told him of one near the hostel and of a youth worker who would befriend him, and put a contact address in the 'Just Grace' booklet. Surely I could do no more?

Six months later I came across him again in the same place. He had not contacted me and I wondered if his conversion had been real. '*I didn't ring you*' he said '*Too busy*'. Disappointment must have shown in my eyes. '*You see, I like to go over to that church over there*'. I looked towards a forbidding mausoleum across the square. '*That's where I like to go and sit – and they had a soup kitchen at Christmas and they know me now. That's where I like to go*'! '*Thank you Lord, you really do look after your new-born lambs*!'

You may think that talking to strangers is easier for me than challenging my friends and you would be right! Well I don't want to lose them, and if they're church friends from the traditional denominations I don't want to rock the boat! Better just to pray for them...? But it was just two such friends who recently invited me round to coffee to hear my testimony. I decided to take the opportunity to ask them the two (diagnostic) questions. What became clear was that although they were devoted to God and their church they had no assurance that the promise of eternal life was really for them. I was surprised and then thrilled as they urged me to continue. I could see the hope in their eyes even as they argued, nervous about accepting God's gift too readily. We discussed the implications of transferring their trust onto Jesus alone. Similarly they were encouraged by learning of the Holy Spirit as a guide or navigator. Eventually they agreed to follow me in prayer that they might have the assurance of eternal life. It was exciting. We then talked about discipleship. Being prayerful churchgoers, they already had a good foundation but we considered how they could develop their personal relationship with Jesus through the Holy Spirit. Our time together ended with grateful prayer and praise. Since then I have seen a joy and a humility in their characters and an effectiveness and power in the way they reach out to others. EE helps people to find assurance in their faith and this allows the Holy Spirit to work more fully in their lives! What a wonderful gift! I can't help wondering how many more there must be in our churches just waiting to be asked!

The great commission is *'Go into all the world...'* and so another amazing thing for me is that within three months of doing the EE training course I was invited to go to Africa! There the training was invaluable and it seemed that everybody wanted to have the gospel explained to them EE style. The 'Just Grace' booklets that I took with me became precious gifts to those converted. Even Moslems came to faith, in spite of the years of dire persecution which might result. I've learnt to be always well provided with 'Just Grace' when travelling abroad as well as at home.

Since that EE course I try to remember to give the smallest outing or encounter to God so that I am ready and willing to be used to share the gospel. I find that the opportunities do not arise unless I make myself available. Then the meetings are never hard and the presentation never difficult. Once I am with someone I ask God to give me love for them and I order the devil to get lost, under my breath of course! Yes EE does take hard work, commitment, planning and prayer and an awareness that God may change your agenda. But what can compare to the joy of sharing the gospel with people and seeing them saved? I just want to shout to the whole world the glory of it!

Diana Home
Diana lives with her husband Gospatric, in Princes Risborough, Buckingham, where they are active members of St Mary's Anglican church. They founded, and continue to run the very successful Christian Resources Exhibitions.

5

A joy and a blessing

I was born on the 20th of February 1957 in Koronadal, South Cotabato, which is a town in the southern part of the Philippines. I lived and worked in the capital city Manila for about nine years before coming to England in October 1989. I came to know the Lord Jesus in April 1983 and have always considered myself as an 'EE Baby' because I was led to the Lord by through an EE gospel presentation.

I was brought up in a religious family and went to a private school run by nuns, but despite the spiritual influences of my family, the church and my school, I never knew God personally. I knew there was a God but he seemed very distant not able to hear our repeated and memorised prayers.

Although part of a big family I grew up feeling nobody really cared for me. I developed an inferiority complex because people always compared me with my sisters. They would say I didn't look like one of the family or I would be mistaken as one of the servants. I became very shy and did not have any self confidence even at school. My mother died suddenly when I was only nine and that affected me very badly. I remember crying in bed every night for a very long time. My misery and sadness became worse when my father married a widow with two children who treated us unfairly. When I went to university it was a relief to get away from home. I joined every organisation, fraternity and sorority group, and hung around with friends but I still felt so lonely inside.

Eventually I ended up getting married at a very young age, hoping that someone might truly care and love me and give me the happiness that I longed for. But I was wrong because we were not prepared for a family. Life was difficult because we were still at college without jobs and depended on our families for support. After three years, my husband was tragically murdered and I was left with a three year old daughter and a newborn son!

Fortunately I had finished my studies just before my husband died and my father helped me get a job in a big government office. I heard of a Bible study going on in another department at lunch break once a week. I enjoyed the studies and was happy with the group where I met Ampy, the lady who organised it.

One lunch break, Ampy shared the good news with me and for the first time in my life I understood the gospel message. I had heard it many times before but the simple way she explained it with simple illustrations made it so clear to me. What touched me most was the realisation that Jesus had died on the cross for ME – for MY sins!, so that I could receive forgiveness and the precious gift of eternal life!!! I was very happy that day and put my trust in Jesus Christ as my Lord and Saviour. My heart was filled with so much love, joy and peace that I never had before. God was no longer distant but someone who is with me all the time. My hopelessness was gone and I was filled with assurance that whatever happens to me, I will be with the One who has loved me more than anybody else in this world.

With excitement I asked Ampy how I could share this good news with my family and friends and she told me about EE. At that time she was training some of the employees who attended the Bible Study. Unfortunately the course was nearly finished so I borrowed some of her training materials because I really wanted to learn how to share the gospel. She invited me to her church for Sunday and even arranged to pick me up. I was amazed at how she cared for me even though I had not known her very long.

That night, I spent hours reading my Bible. I looked up all the references about widows and orphans, read them and even wrote them down. It was so exciting because it was full of promises for me and my children. It was like digging out treasure after treasure and I thought what more could I ask. It was so good to know that God was there for me and would provide whatever was missing in my life. It was a wonderful night of knowing God.

I started learning the EE presentation on my own and also started praying for my family, especially my father and others who were living with us at that time. When I went to church with Ampy for the first time, I was so impressed because the people were so warm and friendly and the service so lively. She told me about the Sunday School so I started taking my children with me every Sunday. Each week I would share with my father or my brother and sisters the good things I learned from church or the Bible study. They started to notice the change in me as I became more happy in my life.

Later on, my younger sister Rowena told me how she had committed her life to the Lord sometime previously when some Christian students shared the gospel with her at university. So she started coming to church with me and my children. One day my youngest sister Merle told me she how she had always wanted to come with us! I sat with her on my bed and started sharing the gospel by using the EE memory cards. She listened with excitement to all that I had to share and then she prayed to receive eternal life. It was a wonderful night because I could feel the presence of the Holy Spirit with us all throughout the night. Then she started coming to church with us and she loved it.

I encouraged my sister Rowena to join the EE training. I wanted to do it but could not make the 16 week commitment because of my children. My sister did the course and has been used by the Lord in so many ways since then. I kept praying that the Lord would also give me the opportunity to be trained.

In January 1985, they announced another programme to start at the end of the month. I really wanted to do it, but could not manage it with the children to look after – so I prayed about it. The week before the course started we received a message from my eldest sister telling us to meet Phoebe. Phoebe told me that she had been my sister's servant for some years and that she had been sent to help me look after my children and the house. What an answer to prayer!! Now I could go do the EE training!

Phoebe used to go to church as a young girl and when I asked her the two EE questions, she answered them correctly! It was exciting to know that she was a Christian and she too started attending church with us. As there were so many of us coming to church Ampy suggested that we hold a home Bible study to help everyone grow and so that the rest of the family could hear the gospel. One night after Bible study an invitation was made and my father, brother and cousin came to know the Lord!

The EE programme started at the end of January 1985 and I was so blessed each week watching my trainer share the gospel and witnessing our contacts pray to receive Jesus as Lord and Saviour. A few weeks later, a Leaders' Training Course was also held at the church and we took the trainees out for their on-the-job training. It was a real joy for me seeing more people led to Christ. While on the training I started praying for my office colleagues and sharing with them as the Spirit led me. It was exciting to see them come to know the Lord and helping them with some discipleship Bible study. I shared with my two children (then aged 5 and 8) and it was a wonderful experience to see them receive eternal life. I also shared with a student who stayed with us at that time and with my cousin who was with us for a few days before she flew to England to get married. I experienced all these people being led to Christ in addition to those we were seeing on our training visits during the course.

That course was one of the most exciting times in my Christian life. I had thought that because of my shyness I would be unable to undertake this ministry, but praise God, He gave me the strength to do it and to overcome my weaknesses. He has blessed me with a special gift of sharing His love with others.

About two years later, the church sent me to be a Sunday missionary to one of our church plants. I started working with a full-time team and each Sunday we would go out with the aim of contacting every house on every street in the area. We shared the gospel with those who welcomed us and followed-up those who made professions of faith. Bible studies were done by the full time workers during the week. It has been a joy to hear that the church planting that we did has now grown to an independent church and those workers have moved on and planted another church. I praise the Lord for the EE ministry and for the perseverance of the believers in my church back in the Philippines. That church has become a centre for EE work, not only training leaders from the Philippines but other Asian countries and some from the Middle East. The programme has been continuously implemented at the church, resulting in rapid growth. The mother church, which started in 1975, now has over twenty daughter churches which are mostly run by young pastors that have come from the congregation. Each year, hundreds of people come to know the Lord and many become missionaries and are sent to other parts of the country and abroad. The church – Kamuning Bible Christian Fellowship (KBCF) – has a vision to be a leading church in missions in the 21st century.

As a widow with two children, I never thought I would marry again. It was a struggle bringing up the children, trying to be father and mother to them, and working hard to meet their needs. One day, my son told me how he wished he had a father, and so we started to pray every night for a father for them – a husband for me. In 1988, I started to receive letters from England! It was a big surprise and I later discovered that my cousin, who came to England to get married, had published my name in a Friendship Club in London. I was not too happy with the idea because if I did marry again I wanted to marry a Christian and thought it would be impossible to meet one in this way. I ignored the first few letters and gave them to some ladies in the office.

One day I received a letter from Robert saying he was a Christian and actively involved with music at his church. I was intrigued by what he said and wrote him a long letter about myself and the children. I also asked him the two EE questions and couldn't wait to get his response. When his reply came, he had answered the questions correctly and I prayed, ' *Lord, is this the answer to our prayers?* ' We started writing regularly for about a year and in February 1989 Robert came to visit us and made a formal proposal. We got engaged and he returned in June for our wedding. Three months later our papers were finally approved and we came to England to join him.

One Sunday morning in 1993, we went to Coton Green Church. The people were friendly, the worship lively and most of all, the Word was preached in a way where I felt fed and blessed. It reminded me of my church back in the Philippines. After a year, we became members and were soon involved in leading worship and Sunday School teaching. But something was missing in this church – there was no evangelism ministry! I started praying because I wanted to be involved again. I talked to one of the leaders about EE and told him what a great benefit it had been to KBCF and the growth of the church as a whole.

Then in 1996, unbeknown to me, Richard, one of the church leaders attended an EE Leaders' Training Course. When he returned he trained two people and I was so surprised when one Sunday morning those two people were awarded their certificates and badges! I knew it was an answer to my prayers. After the service, I went straight to Richard and told him that I would love to be involved in the future. Once again my excitement and love for evangelism was burning in my heart.

In autumn of 1997, Richard asked me to be a trainer for the next programme. I felt inadequate for such a big responsibility because I had not done it for many years, but I knew it was from the Lord. As I started revising from my EE books I became excited as the Lord reminded me of all the experiences I had had in the Philippines and He gave me the strength that I needed. We had six successful trainees on that course. On our first visit I shared the gospel with a couple and their two sons. At the end of it, the whole family gave their hearts to the Lord! This couple subsequently attended our Alpha course. Another lady we visited has also started attending the Alpha course bringing her daughter and other lady friends! We are seeing the results of EE now and it is wonderful to see God move when we obey Him.

My husband enrolled on the next course and was one of my trainees. We have now completed several programmes and there are more than twenty in the church who are trained. The couple who were my first trainees are now in Canada as missionaries.

The EE training is not easy but is always a tremendous blessing to everyone involved, including prayer partners and the contacts. I too am richly blessed as I witness the power of God working in people's lives and have the joy of leading some of them to Christ.

I will never forget Ampy sharing the gospel with me because she cared enough to spend time with me. I want to do the same, not just because Jesus has commanded us to do it, but because I want others to experience the fullness of life in Christ and to have the joy of the assurance of eternal life. By God's grace, I will carry on spreading the good news and hope to pass on to others the love and zeal for evangelism that is truly in my heart.

Elvira L. Calvert
Elvie is married to Robert and they live with four of their children in Tamworth, Staffordshire. They are members of Coton Green Church where Elvie now teaches the EE programme.

6

Not just teaching but reaching

I first became aware of Evangelism Explosion when I was just eleven months old as a Christian – and it has been a very real part of my life ever since. Let me tell you what it has meant to me.

I was teaching in a large secondary school and after the Easter holidays a supply teacher joined the staff for the summer term. She had just returned from Africa where she had served as a Head Teacher for some years. She was very different from me – studious, not very energetic, but despite this we found ourselves getting along in a miraculous way. She was different and this difference was primarily because she had something which I did not have. I began to question her and long discussions followed day after day. She had Jesus as her personal friend and that made all the difference to her, and it was very evident to me. She was confident and peaceful as she went about her daily life.

Then the end of term arrived and I was quite despondent about things and in particular my lack of faith. I rang her on Saturday – she drove over to my home and we went for a walk along the river where our conversation continued. She spoke gently to me about Revelation 3:20 and Jesus standing at the door knocking and then she drove me home and left me to consider this verse and its relevance to me in 1976. At 2:30am I woke and was aware of a Presence in my room. I felt warm, safe and comfortable as I opened the door of my heart and invited Jesus into my life to become my Friend and Guide.

Soon I was offering myself for baptism in the local Baptist church and it was during one of the baptismal classes that the Lord told me quite clearly that He would make me a 'fisher of men'. So it should not have been a surprise to me when one day in December 1977 – on my way out from Sunday morning worship – my Minister said to me, *'I believe you ought to be one of the four trainees in our first EE programme, which begins in about 2 months time.'* Obedient as ever, and unaware of what this would mean or how it would change me, I began the first of many programmes with which have I have been involved in my church.

What did this mean and how did it change me? I am not a studious person, I'd far rather be up and about outside enjoying some form of physical activity – digging, playing badminton – anything rather than settling down to read and study! But this suddenly changed. If I was to become the 'fisher of men' that God had told me I was to be – then I had to learn and find my way around the Bible, a very new but exciting thing for me to embark upon. So began my time as a trainee in Gillingham Baptist Church's first EE programme.

I quickly had to learn to acknowledge God's hand upon my life and to respond to His call in obedience – something which I had found difficult. Being obedient did not come naturally – I thought that I knew best and I was in charge. But change I did and the Lord was ever loving and faithful to me throughout. At first I was complacent but the programme calls for a very disciplined approach and I soon recognised that only 100% of my time and effort would do. The way the learning is broken into 'bite-sized' chunks, plus the encouragement and care of our trainer and fellow trainees helped me enormously. Soon I had settled down to this new discipline. I became more efficient in my use of time, and able to fit into my already full days, time to learn the material, and to study the Bible, plus times of prayer and meditation. This enabled me to grow and slowly mature in my walk of faith.

But these changes were nothing compared to the joy which accompanied them. I soon discovered that this programme was very practical – not restricted to Bible study but getting out into the homes of non-Christians in our community. My fellow trainee and I went into those homes and under the careful eye of our trainer hesitantly and nervously at first, began to 'gossip the gospel' to them. We were soon able to communicate the good news in a clear and direct fashion. Many of the people we visited responded to the offer of God's gift of eternal life and accepted Jesus as their Lord and Saviour – that is where the joy came in. Some of the people who made commitments had been regular churchgoers for many years but, like so many (I have since discovered) had never really understood or been challenged with the need for a personal response.

So, as I learned to communicate the essential truths of the gospel of Jesus, I became a fisher of men. By the end of that first programme I realised that I had been given a wonderful tool. Now, 20 years later, that tool – polished and honed with use – is still very much part of me. It has been, and remains a joy to be able to share the life-changing message of Jesus Christ whenever and wherever the opportunity arises – not just in a programme but in my everyday life. I praise God that He has used me to lead people to Him in all manner of places and situations. This training has enabled me – a very ordinary person – to share Jesus with people – old people, young people and even children. It has allowed me to serve in partnership with Jesus, to bear fruit, fruit that will last – and what a privilege it has been!

I remember one day, sitting quietly in the Coffee Shop (part of the outreach facilities of my church) chatting to an elderly man who was a regular visitor. He was quite amazed to feel loved and cared for by the workers in the coffee shop. This enabled me to tell him how much bigger was the love of God for him. I went on to share the gospel with him, and there and then he reached out to Jesus, offered himself to Him and came to a new understanding of love and forgiveness. Life was not easy for him; he had real problems but he was able to state clearly and openly that having Jesus in his life had made such a difference to him. He understood, perhaps for the first time, that he was valued.

Another memory comes from the first programme. We visited a couple who had been to our church on occasions, but not regularly. Our trainer was not able to be with us – he had an urgent pastoral matter to deal with – so we were alone and nervous. Would we be able to manage and get things in the right place? Our God is ever faithful and at the end of the evening the angels in heaven were rejoicing as all four of us knelt down in the front room and prayed the prayer of commitment together. Twenty years on I still meet in that same room and enjoy fellowship and prayer with that couple – and the husband makes tea for us!

Obviously with people coming to faith my church has also benefited from using the EE programme. Over the years many of our people have been equipped to share their faith. In our first programme – with just two teams – over 30 people made professions of faith – met Jesus for the first time and were soon themselves being trained and then experiencing the joy of leading others to Jesus. The changes in people's lives were very apparent – folks wanted to come to church – no longer a duty but a pleasure to come – to learn and to grow.

In addition to the personal equipping the EE teams have enjoyed the wonderful experience of working closely with others as they have studied, learned, wept and been faithful – together. They have benefited by getting to know other members in a deep and lasting way over the twelve weeks of the learning process. They have experienced a deepening of their own faith and in their understanding of Jesus. Our church has a group of people who are equipped, trained and confident to be obedient to the call to be 'fishers of men'.

Everyone in the kingdom has a story to tell – a story which is as real today as it was when it was written – that Jesus' love is very wonderful and that eternal life is a free gift available to all. How can people believe if they have never heard? They can't! Jesus has told us to GO into all the world and make disciples – to be fishers of men, but just like his first disciples we need to be trained first. The EE programme did that for me – it can do it for you too!

It is a programme which will benefit everyone. Jesus' first group of disciples were ordinary men – but when they were obedient and empowered by the Holy Spirit – they became extraordinary men. This is possible today for ordinary women and men – get on board, learn how to 'gossip the gospel' and experience the peace that passes understanding as you learn and serve the Man called Jesus.

Hazel Mitchell
Hazel is a retired school teacher living in Rainham Kent. She is a member of Gillingham Baptist Church, where she serves as the Sunday School Superintendent and is also on the leadership team. Hazel is also on the Board of Directors of Evangelism Explosion.

7

An unqualified success

I went to church as a young girl although I do not remember to much about it. The thing that stuck in my mind the most was the pretty coloured stickers that we used to get after each Sunday School lesson. I do not remember much about the teaching – they were probably not the most interesting lessons in the world.

We eventually moved to Harlow where I continued to go to Church, and actually had confirmation lessons. By then I was 15 years old and my Mum was expecting her fifth child who was born at the beginning of March. Three weeks later my Mum died. I did not go back to church for many years because I believed that God had taken my Mum away and there was nobody to tell me any different.

It was not until my youngest son started school that I was willing to try church again. Neil and Darren both went to a church school and they went to church for a service once a week. One day after school Darren came out and told me that he had seen Jesus in church. Wow, I thought, my son has had a vision. But in fact he had promoted the vicar to a higher rank! I felt very ashamed that my son did not know the difference between the Vicar and Jesus Christ. So I started to take my sons to church each Sunday and while they went off to Sunday school I would sit in church bored out of my brain.

After about a year three people from the church asked if they could come and see me and talk about their faith. I was a single parent by this time so I was glad of the company. They duly arrived at 8pm and we sat down with a drink. As they shared their faith it was as though a light shone in their faces as they spoke of this person Jesus who obviously had made a big impact on their lives. For the first time in my life, at the age of 33 years, the gospel message made sense and I understood what people meant when they talked about asking Jesus into their lives. Also, after many years of being afraid of death having faced it at a very young age, I understood that if I accepted Christ's wonderful offer of eternal life I need never be afraid again.

The team left me to think about things for three days and came back to see me. Those three days were the most difficult days of my life. But when they returned I knew what I must do and I gave my life to Christ.

I have been working as a pastoral assistant at Christ Church now for about nine years. I have been so blessed by God in all of my work. I am not at all academic but have been teaching EE at the church for at least 18 years. I have lost count of the number of people who have come to faith through the programme. It has to be the easiest way ever to share the gospel so that anyone can understand. It was hearing the gospel in an EE presentation that saved my life and brought me to Jesus. It was the simple but clear way that the team who came were able to present it to me.

As I look back I cannot imagine life without Christ. Bringing up children He was my lifeline. Facing divorce and feeling rejected by someone I loved. Then facing the death of a brother who was only 45 years old – especially when I was asked to take his funeral. But God saw me through that challenging service. He never left my side and with His guidance I was able to share the gospel with over 200 people. Three people came to faith through that service.

I have been able to use the clear EE gospel presentation in all sorts of situations – church services, one-to-one, and even in small groups. I have used it on Baptism visits for many years, where parents really need to understand the gospel before making their baptismal promises before God. And I remember sitting with a group of people on a long train journey from Cornwall when I was asked about my hobbies. I told them that more than anything I enjoyed sharing God's word with people – which I then proceeded to do. At least one person came to faith after that gospel presentation.

I believe that EE is successful because you can learn it and understand it whether you are an academic or you are somebody without much education at all. You can have a go at learning EE, participating in as many programmes as you wish. For the last six years I have taught the programme to some of the most highly qualified people that one can meet at All Nations Christian College. Doctors, nurses, teachers and even vicars! You would be surprised at the ignorance of even those people when it comes to sharing their faith with the ordinary people of this world.

EE also has a unique way of using peoples' personal testimonies – making them down to earth and more natural. Unless you have used it you will never understand the joy of seeing people come to a faith that is everlasting because for the first time in their lives they really understand the gospel message. Once you have learned the presentation you never forget it. You just need to put your personality on it, and make it your own. Then, wherever you go, you have with you one of the most valuable tools that you will ever need.

Jan Young
Jan lives in Ware, Hertfordshire where she works
as pastoral assistant at Christ Church.

8

Open Doors

During 1981, after 15 years of marriage, having had two children, a son aged 11 and a daughter of 9, life seemed to have arrived at a watershed. The realisation that my son was about to start secondary school and in a few short years my daughter too, led me to a growing awareness that they would not need me quite so much and that I needed something more to fill my life.

I was recommended to visit a careers adviser in London and following some aptitude tests it was suggested that I should consider training for a career which involved working with children.

A few more months passed during which time I had an encounter with a lady from Purley Baptist church who was exceedingly kind to me when the Police towed my car away when it was parked on a yellow line! My emptiness was ever more apparent and the need for some form of fulfilment which a kind and generous husband, two lovely children, a beautiful home and numerous possessions could not satisfy.

In October of that year, David, my son, had been at his new school for a month when he came home one afternoon to recount how a school friend had been knocked down by a car on his way to school. This upset me greatly as our local paper had reported two other boys around the age of my son being killed in tragic accidents within the last few months. I felt great sadness that day.

It was a Tuesday, my husband always played Squash on Tuesday evenings. Shortly after he left for the game the doorbell rang.

'Hello, we are visiting from Purley Baptist Church,' the middle-aged lady in the group of three said when I opened the front door. A young woman and young man stood on either side of her. (I later discovered that my visitors were taking part in the Evangelism Explosion training programme at that church.)

'Could we ask you a few questions' she went on, *'for the survey we are conducting?'*

'Oh very well.' I replied. Answer their questions quickly and send them on their way was my thought.

'Do you go to church?'

'No.'

'Have you ever been?'

'Yes, as a child.'

'Do you believe the Bible contains good news for you today?'

'I don't know.'

'Would you be interested in having a personal relationship with God?'

'I'm not sure'

The woman continued: *'May I ask you a personal question?'*

'Well, yes I suppose.'

'If you were to die tonight could you be sure you would go to heaven?'

'I hope so.' I replied.

'If you were to die and stand before God and He was to say 'Why should I let you into my heaven?' what would you say?'

'Well, I have lived a good life, I have done as much as I could to help people and to be kind.'

I began to feel uneasy – dying – standing before God? What was this all about? This was all becoming too personal.

'I'm sorry,' I said *'It's very late, I have answered your questions and really don't want to answer any more.'*

I was surprised that I was so rude and abrupt. I was usually more tolerant than this but these people were beginning to get to me. I wasn't sure why I was feeling quite like I was but I wanted them to go. Then, suddenly the young woman in the group began to speak:

'Do you remember reading recently about a boy who was riding his bike, he overtook his friend and was knocked down by a car driving toward them and was killed?

'Yes, yes, I do remember that.' I said.

'That boy was my brother.'

A chill went straight through me as I recalled David's school friend lying in intensive care at Atkinson Morley Hospital having been knocked down that very morning.

She went on, *'I know my brother is in heaven and I will see him again one day.'*

I knew by the way she spoke she believed this to be true. I also knew this was something I could not ignore. This was God and He was speaking directly to me. It was as if He had hold of me by the shoulders and was shaking me into an awareness of Him. I knew I could not dismiss anything these people had to tell me.

I suddenly changed from a cold, distant person to a desperate woman needing to hear what they had to say. I invited them into the house but the leader of the team suggested they return the following week as it was now rather late. My appetite was well and truly whetted and I was disappointed that they had declined my offer to come in there and then and to explain more. With hindsight, however, I believe it showed great wisdom.

The following week was very strange. I was on tenterhooks the whole time – afraid that they would not return, but of course they did. I was like a dry sponge and just soaked up the entire gospel. I read everything they gave me. Over the next few weeks I continued to read and ask questions. I became increasingly aware that there was something I had to do and was eager to discover the final necessary step I had to take. Pam (the middle-aged lady) did not rush anything and I was literally champing at the bit when she brought me to the point of commitment. As I prayed with them, repenting of my sins, I was born again, and the joy which filled me was beyond measure. I was totally elated – I had come home, to the place I had been seeking all my life. Later that day I remember collecting my daughter from school and being so excited that when she got into the car I just told her everything. My darling nine year old daughter evangelised to all her class mates over the next few weeks.

I was aware that I had total peace and satisfaction in having found Jesus as my Saviour and Lord and felt that was it, life was complete and we would all live happily ever after.

A few weeks later in the local paper I saw an advertisement for a part-time Bachelor of Education course at the Polytechnic of the Southbank. This was everything I had been looking for originally but had never found – the opportunity to become a school teacher. I can remember having an argument with the Lord telling Him that now I had Him I did not need anything else. Yet I was aware that I must pursue this as it was a possible open door that He had created and therefore one which I could not ignore. I prayed that if it was not His will then I would not get onto the course. I did get onto the course and was there for four years.

During that time I became a member of Purley Baptist church and, wanting to tell my friends and family about my new-found faith took the opportunity to be trained in Evangelism Explosion. I used EE regularly, not only when visiting people in the neighbourhood but also at College. Everyone heard from me whenever there was an opportunity to get alongside someone and speak, even the college lecturers heard about Jesus. I met with other Christians on the course and we formed a prayer group, praying for other students and for our own needs within the College. All of this was so worthwhile but as finals approached I thought my involvement in education might be at an end. However, God had other plans. I passed the finals and became a teacher.

Years passed and through my work with children there were many opportunities to show my love of Jesus, to the children, to parents, to teacher colleagues and to the many others with whom I came into contact. I continued visiting and sharing the gospel of Christ within the locality as well.

Following retirement from school the Lord has shown me a new work He has prepared for me involving many different strands. Some of this work takes me into the homes of shut-ins where I not only listen but am able to point them to Jesus. I also attend various non-Christian groups locally where opportunities frequently arise to share God's love .

I am so grateful for my EE training which has provided a sound structure for presenting the gospel. Wherever I am and whatever I am involved in, no matter how many 'red herrings' may come up during a conversation, it is possible to link into where the people are and so direct them to Jesus and the cross.

How much people just want to talk and be listened to and how white the fields are for harvest. God has provided open doors for us to go into the world and express His love for humanity through our active service. Part of this service is befriending and loving people with the love of Jesus, meeting their needs and introducing them to the Saviour of the World.

Pat Jane
Pat lives with her husband in Ashtead,, Surrey and is an active member of St George's Anglican church.

9

From diffidence to confidence

In October 1982 our family moved to a Baptist church which, after 50 years with the Brethren, was a big change. Zion Baptist is a lovely, warm, caring church, with an openness to the Holy Spirit which came as a balm to my soul.

As long as I can remember, I had had a low opinion of myself and my capabilities, and never felt evangelism was one of my gifts. But I was asked to be a prayer partner for the first Evangelism Explosion team trained at Zion, and felt very honoured. Later, after hearing God say to me, *'You will be my witness'* at an Arthur Blessitt meeting, I agreed to do the training myself. On our very first visit two young people came to the Lord.

That EE training unlocked something in timid, insecure, diffident me! I grew in confidence doing things I had never thought that I would. It was delightful as, one by one, I began to see people coming to faith.

Others in the church recognised my new-found confidence and in January 1986, after attending a six-day Leaders' Training Course at

Abertridwr in South Wales, I was asked to take over the leadership of the EE programme at Zion. The enemy tried to prevent this, as I broke my left arm three weeks before that training course. But he got it wrong because I am right-handed!

I leaned hard on the Lord at that time, as I had never really led anything before. I also leant on my Pastor and prayer partners too. We wept many tears, prayed much, and laughed as well but what a difference that training made – and not just to me!

One day in church I noticed a lady, about my age, whom I had not seen before. I went to speak to her and she told me how she had suddenly felt she wanted to go to church, but didn't know anything about Baptists. I offered to call on her and explain. She wanted this and our friendship began. At last I felt she was ready for a presentation of the gospel, and took my trainees round. She responded gloriously amid many tears. Later she said, *'I feel three stone lighter!'* She was baptised six months later to my utter joy, and the next week began her EE training. I have heard her say that that was the time of her life when she learnt most, and really progressed in the knowledge of her Lord.

Another contact we made was a young woman who came to 'Keep Fit' which we held at the church. She was a single mum expecting her second child. Eventually we visited her. By then we knew her quite well and at her request, had already prayed for her baby to be born normally, as she had a suspected placenta praevia. He was! I think we had a record number of visits to her house going there six times or more. One night we said not a word of the gospel, but held the baby while the doctor came to see her other child. Chaos reigned that night but a firm friendship was formed. We had presented the gospel, answered many questions that she had, and she had still not made a response – but the way had been prepared! One evening in church, she plonked her baby in the arms of an elderly spinster and went forward to accept Jesus. She too subsequently trained in EE and although struggling with arthritis and with two teenagers to bring up, maintains her faith in the Lord.

One day at the toddler group two little girls were brought in by their step-grandmother – (R). She looked rather lonely so I went over to chat with her. She was a very worried lady, having had tests at the hospital which showed a large mass in her abdomen. I had had similar tests so we talked about it together and she let me pray for her there. Some time later a mutual friend phoned to say that 'R' had only two weeks to live and would I visit her as the friend wasn't sure if 'R' knew Jesus personally. I felt the enormity of the responsibility so I asked the friend to pray with me, which he did. The next day I visited 'R' and could see she was a very sick lady. She was very frightened, but we had both been nurses so we talked openly about it all, understanding what it could mean. *'Eternity is such along time,'* she said. I shared the gospel with her and she listened eagerly. Leaving her a 'Just Grace' booklet, I left just as the nurse arrived. All the way home I struggled and wept because I hadn't led her through to faith. Then I felt the Lord say to me, *'it is all in My hands, I am in control here, rest it with Me.'* So I did. When I phoned 'R' a few days later she wanted me to call again. This time I shared the gospel again and led her to put her faith in Jesus. I drove home rejoicing. A week later when I called her husband said that she was much better! She was eating and sleeping and much happier. When we talked she said, *'The fear is gone. I couldn't understand why I felt so much better until I remembered the prayer I prayed last week!'* I visited a few more times, reading and praying and even singing to the Lord. She seemed so much better in every way that I did wonder if the Lord had healed her body as well as her soul. The last time I saw her she was planning a holiday to visit her daughter. Some weeks later I heard she had passed away. Although I felt I had lost a dear friend, how wonderful to know she is in heaven with the Lord, and one day we will meet again.

A great joy is equipping others to do this vital work. I was due to go on holiday in March 1998 and this was the last evening the team would meet together. We had one trainee and two people who had just completed their training. A visit had been arranged but I had a streaming cold and neither of them felt confident to lead a team on their own. However, they agreed to go together with the one trainee. On their return I could hardly contain my joy as I heard how they had led a young woman to Jesus! Wonderful as it is to have that privilege oneself – to know that these two people were now able to do it, was even better.

One of the things I like to see is a number of people involved in the work, both in and out of EE. Recently a young man helped a church member to move house. He had helped her on a number of occasions as she was a single mum in rented accommodation and had often moved. He had noticed a real change in her life when she came back to the Lord after a 'drifting' time. He also talked with many other Christians who were helping her, asking many questions as they painted walls! One night, when she was to give her testimony in church, he came along to listen.

He kept on coming, and eventually we arranged to visit him. We were able to present the whole gospel and he eagerly and tearfully responded. We were very much aware, however, that the EE team were only three among many who had been instrumental in his conversion.

That of course is the secret – it is a work of the Spirit of God entirely and we are His instruments. He uses us and as we wield the tool of EE by the power of God we are privileged to see lives touched and changed. I am so grateful to Him that I have had so many opportunities to share the gospel, to lead people to Jesus, to train others, and to learn to trust Him more.

Mrs Peggy Darch

Peggy lives with her husband Ken on their farm near Taunton, Somerset. She is an active member of the pastoral team at Zion Baptist Church in Creech St Michael, Taunton, where until very recently, she was responsible for the EE programme.

10

A tool for life – eternal life

Like many people who come to faith as an adult, I had a burning desire to tell others of this new found treasure – the pearl of great price. I had the zeal and, as an insurance rep., any number of opportunities to share with unsaved friends and contacts – but I saw no fruit. However, I still had that desire to share my faith with others and, together with a friend in the church, planned to do some door-to-door work. We took the idea to the pastor who praised our enthusiasm but very wisely suggested that we should first get some appropriate training. He suggested Evangelism Explosion. This was back in the early eighties and neither of us had heard of it. He told us that a church in a neighbouring town was running a programme and arranged for us to be included. What an amazing time that was!

The training then ran over seventeen weeks and by the end of it my Christian witness had been revolutionised. Since coming to faith some seven years previously I had been privileged to enjoy excellent Bible teaching and preaching at the local church and was a really keen Bible student. But not all the sermons I had heard, nor the many Christian seminars I had attended, nor the countless Christian books I read, gave me what I received from that course. It was so practical, and so comprehensive that, by the end of it, I realised that I had not only been given a superb tool to share the gospel, but had gained an understanding of my faith as never before. Since that course I praise God that I have had the joy of sharing the gospel with hundreds of people on a one-to-one basis and leading many of them to a saving faith in Jesus. Here are a just two stories that highlight the significance of this training for me.

A couple of years after my initial EE training the mother of a very close friend was admitted to a local hospice. What was thought to have been just a 'back problem' had turned out to be terminal cancer. Although Claire and her husband were Christians 'mum' wasn't and they asked me to visit her with the express purpose of sharing the gospel. This was quite a challenge. Although by this time, I had presented the gospel on many occasions this would be different. Claire's mother was fading fast so there was an urgency here – literally a matter of eternal life or death. Without EE where would I have begun. Without it of course I wouldn't have been asked, but I had been trained and was ready to help these dear friends. Having first got her answers to the two diagnostic questions Claire's mother listened with rapt attention as I presented the gospel, telling her the good news of God's amazing gift. It made sense to her and right there in that hospice ward we bowed in prayer as she committed her life to Jesus. Claire and her husband had been praying at home and were delighted to get the news. Understandably perhaps, we asked ourselves was this commitment real? We soon had our answer. When they visited her later that day her eyes were shining as never before – and from this and the things she said they knew it was real. A couple of days later Claire's mother died but we were able to rejoice in the knowledge that she had passed from death to life.

On another occasion I was sitting in the back row of a church when a young man came in and sat down a couple of seats away from me. He clearly enjoyed the service, singing the hymns and choruses very enthusiastically, even to the extent of raising his hands – like many others in that congregation. At the end of the service I discovered that he had recently moved into the area and, being a regular church-attender, was looking for a suitable church. As we continued to talk I felt it right, in spite of his obvious familiarity with church, to ask him the diagnostic questions. I am glad I did, for though he knew *about* Jesus he didn't know Him personally. There, at the back of the church, I presented the gospel and led him into a personal relationship with the Lord.

These are just two examples among many where that clear gospel presentation not only made sense but made the difference. In the case of the young man at the back of the church, without those two questions I would not have been able to 'diagnose' his situation, let alone have the temerity to ask them! And what about Claire's mother? Her children may have asked a minister to visit her but would that have guaranteed that she heard the gospel in a way that made sense? I am not so sure, for whilst ministers find no difficulty in presenting the gospel from the pulpit many freely admit that it is an altogether different matter when sharing one-to-one.

Peter Crook, National Director, Evangelism Explosion

For most of his life Peter worked for an insurance company before taking over as National Director of EE in the UK in 1991. He is married and currently lives in Taunton, Somerset where he and his wife are members of Zion Baptist Church.

82

11

David, please teach us to evangelise!

Those words put my mind into a whirl. It was 1975 and Gilly (my wife) and I had been at Christ Church, Barking for three years. Following a three year curacy at Christ Church, North Finchley, during which time we had learned about and experienced new power through the work of the Holy Spirit, we were now living on a self-contained council estate of 8,000 people. As Team Vicar I was leading a small but lively congregation. Every Friday evening a group of about seven of us met in our vicarage to pray. It was on one of those occasions that the request was made.

Early in my ministry I had enjoyed talking about Jesus, but had not found it easy to present the gospel clearly, and had certainly not seen anyone receive Christ directly through my witness. That had changed when we experienced more of the power of the Spirit though I was still very reliant on booklets such as 'Journey into Life'. In Barking I had seen plenty of encouragement, especially as a result of Infant Baptism contacts. With God's help I was able to lead a few people to Christ. For me personally evangelism was not the problem it once had been. However the request the prayer group made was not for me to evangelise, but to teach them to do so. That was quite a different matter. How could I teach something in which I was so inexperienced and hesitant about myself? I went into my study and gathered all the books and courses in evangelism I had, laying them out on our sitting room floor for the seven of us to look at. Amongst them was a book on Evangelism Explosion. I had heard about EE just two weeks previously from the Rev David Bubbers, at that time Vicar of Emmanuel, Northwood. I had liked what I had heard. Now as we looked at all the options, EE was the unanimous choice. But what was to be the next step? There were no Leaders' Training Courses in this country at that time and no teaching materials.

Receiving information from Northwood I planned a twelve week course of our own. Every week Gilly and I would learn the next chapter, teach it and take the others out on visits. Talk about the blind leading the blind! However, though we did not see any commitments, we had some excellent visits and our enthusiasm grew. Soon there was a promotional meeting held in London with Archie Parrish from Coral Ridge Presbyterian Church. That was the clincher and four of us booked in for the first two 'Clinics' (Leaders Training Courses) held at Northwood and Corby. Things have never been the same since!

I went to the Clinic at Emmanuel, Northwood. By then, we had a reasonable grasp of the material but were longing to see commitments. I was certainly hoping to see at least one during the on-the-job training on the Clinic. I was to be disappointed over that but over nothing else. That Clinic changed my ministry. Not only was I able to spend time really learning the material but I learned a great deal from the visits. Another minister and myself were trained by an eighteen year old girl who had never been a trainer before. She was great. Above all I learned from her the value of not being deflected from the overriding purpose of sharing the gospel. She was nothing if not determined. I will always be grateful to her.

The two days following the Clinic were among the most exciting in my life. I had gone hoping to see some commitments but our team had seen none. I think God saved them all up for my return to Barking. Seven people accepted Christ in those two days! They were all thrilling stories, but for me the most moving was of Pam's mother. Pam worshipped at the main parish church and her mother was ill with cancer. I only knew Pam by name and the illness of her mother had only vaguely registered with me so that when I came across her on my hospital round I did not give it a second thought. What I did do was to ask the lady the 'two questions' and share the gospel with her. She received eternal life. I left her with a booklet, promising to return the following week. When I did I found that she had left hospital so on the following day I went to her home. The door was opened by Geoff, Pam's husband. Pam's mother had died that morning. That was not the end of the story. A little later I had a phone call from the family. Would I speak at the funeral service please. I did. The day after the funeral another phone call. This time, would I go and see Pam and her husband. They did not know what I said to their mother, but it had made so much difference to the last week of her life that they wanted to hear it themselves. At that visit Pam too received eternal life.

I have often wondered about that hospital visit. If I had known Pam's mother was dying of cancer when I first saw her in hospital, would I have been more hesitant to ask her whether she was certain she was going to heaven? If that had been the case she might not have received God's wonderful gift. A big lesson learned. Those questions are very important in all circumstances.

Now that we were better equipped to train others we soon had the privilege of seeing church members leading others to Christ. There was Val who in her first course as a trainer led more people to Christ than the rest of us put together. She had not been able to share the gospel before. Then there was Rae, a senior member of our sister church. A lifetime of church membership had not given her assurance of salvation – an EE gospel presentation did! Rae did not find the learning easy but two courses later she returned from a visit with a broad grin on her face. She had led someone to Christ for the first time in her life. If there is a greater thrill than leading someone to Christ it is seeing someone you have trained do so.

During the next five years we not only trained members of Christ Church in EE, but also members of three other Anglican churches and of the local Elim church. That resulted in the Elim Church adopting EE in their training and the Pastor, Brian Richardson subsequently becoming Chairman of EE(GB). It also made a big impact on those we visited who were struck by the fact that churches were working so closely together. This was also a big factor after we had moved to St. Clement's, Toxteth Liverpool in 1981. EE was just as effective for training in our riot-hit parish there as it had been in Barking. We then had the privilege of leading a course with trainees from the eleven churches of the

Toxteth Evangelical Fellowship. It is good to know that some of those trained are still using EE today.

In 1991 we moved to St. Peter's Parr, in St. Helens, Merseyside. There was no need to introduce EE here. It had been faithfully maintained here since 1976. At that time the Rector, Rev John Roberts began the EE training when he was challenged personally by Ezekiel 33:6 *'But if the watchman sees the sword coming and does not blow the trumpet to warn the people and the sword comes and takes the life of one of them, that man will be taken away because of his sin, but I will hold the watchman accountable for his blood'*. Because John faced up to the challenge, not only of 'sounding the trumpet' himself but of training others to do the same, many people here have been trained and many have come to know the Lord through their witness. It is a challenge we all face as ministers. I have found no better method of fulfilling our responsibilities than by using the Evangelism Explosion witness training programme.

Rev David Thompson
David is vicar of St Peter's and the team rector of the parish of Parr, St Helens, where he lives with his wife Gilly. He is also chairman of the Board of Directors of EE.

??

To discover how you can be sure of eternal life, see page 92

To discover more about the Evangelism Explosion training programme, see pages 90, 91

??

Evangelism Explosion

What it is: It is a 12-week apprenticeship-style training programme in personal evangelism. Its purpose is to equip Christians to present the gospel in a simple, clear and sensitive manner. In addition participants learn how to handle objections, lead a person to Christ, disciple new believers and help train others in the church to do the same.

Where it came from: It started in the early sixties in a small Presbyterian church in Florida. The minister, Dr D. James Kennedy was a gifted preacher, well able to present the gospel from the pulpit, but found personal witnessing very difficult. Then, whilst taking part in a mission in a neighbouring State, he was *'shown how to do it'*. Developing what he had learned, he put together the Evangelism Explosion training programme for his church. As a result that small church grew rapidly and today has a membership in excess of 8,000. Other churches soon took up the programme and by the end of 1995 it had reached every nation of the world.

EE(GB) has been established in the UK since 1975.

How it works: Those taking part meet together for a weekly study session, which lasts about an hour, to learn a comprehensive gospel presentation. Following the study session they divide into teams of three *(an experienced trainer with two trainees)* for *on-the-job training.* They visit homes in the neighbourhood where they see in practice what they have been learning in theory. Over the weeks, as the trainees grow in confidence, they are encouraged to take an increasingly greater part in presenting the gospel. In due course, and often well before the end of the 12 weeks, they are ready and able to share their faith, within the programme or in the everyday opportunities of life.

How to get EE started at your church: The first step is to get one or more of your leaders trained at a six-day Leaders' Training Course. A number of these courses are held each year around the country at churches where the EE ministry is established. During the intensive, six-day course, (which includes on-the-job training) participants cover all the EE material. Subject to reaching a satisfactory standard of competence, they will then be in a position to commence the training in their own churches.

For details of courses, application forms and further information contact the EE Office in Southampton: address on back page.

Eternal Life and The Two Questions

You may have noticed that many of the contributors to this booklet refer to 'two questions' or the 'diagnostic questions*', and that they also mention their *assurance* of eternal life. (ie the assurance they have that when they die they will go to heaven to live with God forever.) This *assurance* is the subject of the first of the two questions, which asks,

> *'Do you know for certain that if you were to die tonight you will go to heaven?'*

If you don't have this assurance you can, for the Bible says that these things are written '...*that you may KNOW that you have eternal life*' (1 John 5:13).

The second question may need a little more reflection. It is:

> *'If you were to die and stand before God and He were to ask you, 'Why should I let you into my heaven' what would you say?'*

If you are unsure as to the answers to these questions and would like to know for certain that you have eternal life then please contact the EE office for a copy of the *Just Grace* booklet (see address on back page), or you can purchase a copy from your local Christian bookshop.

*(These two questions are fundamental to the EE presentation of the gospel.)

The EE discipleship training programme is specifically designed to enable the local church to train and equip its members for effective personal witnessing.

Evangelism Explosion (GB)
PO Box 552, SOUTHAMPTON, SO18 1ZL
Tel/Fax: 023 80228985
visit our web site at www.ee-gb.org.uk

Evangelism Explosion (GB) Ltd
is a charity registered in England No 269722

Evangelism Explosion

Making sense to make a difference in every nation of the world!